To LYN Patric

IRAQI HEADACHES

We Tazz Juru

we die soon

Be Positive

IRAQI HEADACHES

POEMS BY
SAIF ALSAEGH

NOUVEAU NOSTALGIA
GREAT FALLS, MONTANA

Published by Nouveau Nostalgia
Great Falls, Montana
nouveaunostalgia.com

ISBN 978-0-9912884-0-3

Cover and interior design by Sara Habein and Tyson Habein
Edited by Sara Habein and Ziad Al-Shamsie
Arabic translations by Saif Alsaegh
Typeset in Harting and Latin Modern Mono:
fontsquirrel.com

Printed by 48 Hour Books
Akron, Ohio
48hourbooks.com

This book is not an attempt to change the world.
In fact, it will leave it empty...

...as it has always been.

Find yourself in a country where there is only the sea.

CONTENTS

ONE

To Rimbaud, Baudelaire and Rock 'n' Roll

I was young
I was mad
I went far
looked at the sea, the people
and decided to go to war.

Filthy City
(To used condoms on the streets of Brooklyn)

The City is filthy
people walking with bottles of gin,
in circles.

Tall buildings masturbating
on the history of ancient battles.
Men of three legs
women of no lipstick.

Black parties
photographs of dying couples
all eyes illuminating
all souls naked.

Libraries filled with the smoke of nothingness.
Paved roads
miles and miles of paved roads,
immigrants' grocery stores.
Cathedrals
eating the lonely smiles of their children.
In the city there are

Facts:

Breathing is dangerous.
Hell is here, in our brains.
Airplanes are always sad.
We're alone in this world.

Discoveries:

Better than music
better than fire
like the misty mountains at sunset
words of dead poets.

Happiness generates emptiness,
Jesus said.

Mother Mary was not a virgin.

History is a myth.

I'm not the man of God anymore.

Random scenes:

Strangers
in a bar
burning the illusion of existence.

Drunk men under a bridge
creating their own heaven.

A father telling his daughter
how sad she'll grow up to be.

O City filled with filth
bottles of gin and people walking in circles
wishing they were dead.

I want to tell you:

I'm just like you

I'm not sad

I'm not dead

I'm just trying to find eternity in my reflection.

A Song
(To the ones who drowned in holy water)

GOD: Here, come over here.

ME: O God, your face is unknown to the painters.
Poets are not prophets.

GOD: Here, come over here.

ME: Where do I find the truth?

GOD: In wastebaskets.

ME: Not even in the heart of the sea?

GOD: In wastebaskets.

Son of Nothingness
(To myself, the son of a liberty pimp)

I'm the son of every cursed poet
I'm the son of every suicidal soul
I'm the son of the non-famous brilliants
I'm the son of the ones who burned their cross.

Groups of people cheering loudly, celebrating the
chaos
Food, alcohol, empty conversations
Groups of people are hideous.

Can you see Jesus walking between the night-kill-
ers?
Can you see every torn-hearted mother praying
through cold nights while God sleeps?
Can you feel the woman with cold skin?

Faces engraved with sad expressions
Smiles hidden under the dooms of night
Bars with no alcohol
Empty motel rooms.

I'm the son of the ones who gave up
I'm the son of painters who sold their unframed
souls for $4.99 and bought
the heavens hidden in a joint.

Can you see the doors open?
Can you see the foggy path to the new world?

Black holes, swallowing the air in our lungs
eating the homeless children
leaving the lonesome evenings suffocating.

I'm the son of ancient bridges
I'm the son of gunpowder
I'm the son of dirty fantasies
I'm the son of distraction
I'm the son of hallucinations

I'm the son of the drug addicts and the insane who
laughed at people and walked away

Can you see the light burning the hanged days?
Can you feel your heartbeats slowing down?
Can you hear the silence?
Can you see the end?

I'm the son of everything that never existed
I'm the son of nothingness.

Ruins
(To Baghdad, where I died many times)

BOOM!

                    The sky is vomiting dying infants.
                                        BOOM!

Baby, cover me with your eyelashes.
BOOM!

                    I'm intoxicated with gunpowder.
                                        BOOM!

The old people are swollen with insanity.
BOOM!
            The mothers are sacrificing their children
                                    to the sun.
                                        BOOM!

Fire doesn't kill me anymore.
BOOM!

        Another report says: we're going to die soon.
                                        BOOM!

I leave my gun to a dead body in the river.
BOOM!
                    I hide under the ruins of my house
                            Smoke my last cigarette
                            Shoot my dream in the head.

Orgasm of NYC
(To dreams on dirty pillows)

I remember how the dawn was tickling my soft hands.
Buildings, subways, all leading to the small apart-
ments and unwanted meetings. Have you walked Manhat-
tan at 6 a.m.? The mystical lights, all the faces,
tired and filled with millions of bad photographs.
All the grandmothers and the grandfathers. New York
City is filled with children. Death is close to their
skin, to their majestic eyes, to their dreams, to the
sunshine covering their bodies. It is close to each
and every one of them.

A Song About a Stuffed Rainbow
(To a mummified hippie)

Sing, babies are being born
China is a billion people
We love wars.

Sing, small rooms crammed with people
Music is real
No one prays to God.

Sing, we died today
The night was heavy
Jesus died for our innocent sins.

Sing, a million women pregnant
The lights never sleep
The world is a headache.

Sing, when the drums speak
Rivers and clouds smile
On our deserted paradise.

Sing, Time is a matter of old watches
Future doesn't exist
Alcohol is the answer.

Sing, mama smiled a lot
When she cut our fingernails
Sleeping in cold rooms.

Sing, when porn stars were featured on
The Pope's forehead,
The people danced.

Sing, I don't believe in sleeping early
Songs are nightmares
Insomnia is your paradise.

Sing, I slept with her
She was crying
I hate her cancer.

Sing, in New York
There's one tree
And too many people.

Sing, between every other line
I haiku
Fuck poetry.

Sing
Sing
Keep Singing
Die alone.

Half Bodies
(To Baghdad's chaotic map of AK-47s)

It was not a sunny day
Dry weather as we walked to our death
Calm, vivid blue
Pushing our scrap wagon
Reminiscing laughs
So loud was our screaming
as we cursed the past.

We tried to run away
Leaving the remains of civilization
Lonesome between the ancient gods
of light, sex, love.

The bridge, closed.
Concrete walls caged our hearts
Blurry images of the old days scattered 'round
It's just another day
of looking at the closed bridge.

We didn't care
as we decided to stay in the map
without oxygen
Gazing at the sky
with our half bodies.

American Nightmares
(To the American False Dream)

America is pregnant.
America is silent.
America is filled with sad families.
Yes, Mommy, I hate myself.

America is
at the door
Soldiers are knocking
asking politely:
Can we kill you?

America is suicidal
when the streets are empty
America is a bottle of alcohol
in the lonely playgrounds

America is a bloodstain
on Kabul's children's clothes

America cooks meth through gun barrels!

America, why don't you love me?
America, why are your legs shaking?
Do you know how the long-bearded men feel at night?
Do you know how many teenagers have stopped hoping?

America is insane
America doesn't sleep at night

America, why don't you believe in dawn?

Your old buildings are falling down
Your beautiful ladies are aging
Your nuclear missiles are getting ugly

America, why don't you love me?

America, the sun doesn't rise
America, my father loved the river more than me
America, my toys are broken
America, I'm not brave
America, the dark, dying diners
America, the sounds of bombs
America, the world's maps are crying
America, don't hide in a corner
America, don't you put on too much make-up
America, why don't you love me?
America, why do you hate yourself?

Throne of Grace
(To the prayers of a sad frog)

Every day I sit on the edge of eternity
I gaze at the sky filled with naked women
for hours and hours and hours
I watch God paint graffiti with the children's
tears
Then I howl with a sick revolution
Read poetry under a dirty blanket
On a bed made of words and magic
I drink the alcohol given to me by
a lonesome monster with three golden wings

Tell me
How can we burn the throne of grace?
How can we scream in the face of the Earth with no
fear?
How can we kill ourselves with water guns?

Every day I sit on the edge of eternity
burning a brain filled with jasmine
and crazy ideas
Paintings of every poet who never saw the ocean
and every man who never fell in love

How can we burn the throne of grace?

Every day I sit on the edge of eternity
Seeing humanity's small dreams
And how they can fill millions of books
Books with no words
Books of music
Books jammed with prayers
Prayers of teenagers who wake up early every day
just to see the sunrise
Prayers of all the hipsters who wander the streets
alone at night
Prayers of mothers who sing endlessly

Tell me
How can we burn the throne of grace?
How can we strangle our dreams with laughter?

Every day I sit on the edge of eternity
and decide not to be a god
Because I shine more than the light
In my veins, a million stars make love
and infinite dreams have
The nasty urge to burn the throne of grace.

Breathe
(Find yourself rotten)

I live here
With all the Hindu symbols reminding me I'm incomplete
A dirty poster of Tyler Durden hangs loosely on the
wall

I live here
With my dying sperm
With a sad song
I lay down and think of dreams
My veins turning into rivers, leading to mushroom
fields,
hallucinating wisdom

I make tea in the afternoon
Watch people from the window
Some dance, some fight, the rest die slowly like a
lonesome beast

We're born here
from a copy machine
To breathe
with no significance.

Beautiful Poems
(To old poetry books buried in the graveyard
of insanity)

HIM: What are you doing these days?

ME: Nothing. Just reading poems, writing poems,
editing poems, sleeping with poems,
hugging poems, eating poems, drinking poems,
peeing poems, killing poems, dreaming poems,
singing poems, talking to poems...

HIM: So?!!

ME: I don't like it. Poems are ugly.

The Bohemian Man
(To Seattle grunge and suicide)

I see
Rock 'n roll moving his skinny fingers
Old, trembling
Softly touching the newspaper
Skimming headlines
Stopping at colorful photos.

A long-bearded man
White like a dead angel
Bald like the world.
He reads a sarcastic cartoon
Eats a cookie from a dirty plastic bag.
He gazes at his red backpack
Readjusts his *We are the 99%* button

Folds the newspaper
Looks at the pile of books in this small café
Moves his head to the music
Back and forth, like the wind
And like a small cloud he shuts his eyes and
Sleeps.

He's lonely
Lonelier than God

He's sad
Sadder than me.

Happy Birthday
(To angels with no birthdays)

Okay,
He is coming. Dim the restroom light, the kitchen
light, the moon light.
3, 2, 1

Surprise.

To you my soul
To every nerve in my fingers that sang
sterile poems
To wretches who kept talking to the streets through
poetry
To the beggar I captured with my camera in Boston
To the lonesome who kept masturbating to forget
To the eighty-year-olds who died and never found
paradise
To employees choking themselves with neckties

Surprise.

To Fady, the first name of a miracle gods neglected
To Kurt Cobain, why did you kill yourself?
To Allen Ginsberg, to Charles Manson
To the old man living in an empty house with one
chair and two blankets
To the fat who run on the treadmill every day and
never lose weight
To the kids who see meat every day and
never taste it

To the shy adolescent who didn't talk to the girl
he liked
because he was told not to dream
To the insane eating the holy dirt and cursing the
sun that burned their skin
To the night walkers sitting on benches watching
the train as they see everything fades away
To the tall black men who threw a thousand balls
and never scored
To the runners
To gays
To non-gays
To non-straight
To the queer... to the questioning

Surprise.

To my sisters
To all girls who stuff their bras
It's okay; I'll give you my penis
Create a new gender
Mix it, shake it
Make it revolutionary.
To the witty politicians
To the stupid majority
To cheap songs
To yellow cabs flying like angels on 42nd Street

To spiritual vaginas
To the hookers in the Middle East
To the priests and imams
To you my soul

Surprise.

To jumping thoughts
To my insomnia
To books I've never read
To the wind that reminds me of x-girlfriends
To documentaries that made me cry
To dad, mom, uncle, aunt
To Catholics, Muslims, Evangelicals, Atheists
To the two bottles of beer on my floor that keep
cursing the Almighty

Surprise.

To the words I love:

Good, Nice, Fuck, Shit, Bitch, Motherfucker,
Vodka, Peace, Orgasms, Porn, Tit job, Blow job,
Beer,
Fries

Surprise.

To cities I loved

To Istanbul where I should have had sex
To Damascus where I should have had sex
To New York where I should have had sex
To Denver where I should have had sex
To Boston where should I have smoked weed
To Oakland where I should have died
To Seattle where I should have cried, smoked, died
and had sex   37

Surprise.

To pages and pages of nonsense
To the holy poems of death
To the neverlands
To the alarm clock
To the heaven that I'll see from far away

Surprise.

To the languages I will never learn:
Arabic, English, French, Assyrian, Spanish,
Italian, Hebrew, Kurdish, Turkish, Dutch, Japanese
and the divine languages of India.

Surprise.

To freedom
To diet coke
To the food I miss
To killers and rapists
To the bathroom cleaners
To the librarians
To infamous painters and poets working day and
night in my brain
To the cup of coffee I drink every morning and
never liked

To the faded blue
To the blue of spirit
To the blue of her underwear
To her red nail polish

To country music
To jails
To cigarettes
To the saxophone calling God under the rainy
streets

Surprise.

To smoking pot
To reading newspapers
To drinking iced tea
To fucking wives
To fucking other women besides wives

To cursing God
To praising God
To reading
To writing
To crying
To dying
To you my soul

Surprise.

Horizon
(To Dihya, the Queen of Berber)

I wear my shades and smoke a cigar
Could you tell me how she fell in love with me?
I'm yellow green
Pale most of the day
I'm a gloomy country singer
I'm a black and white laughing cartoon
Nothing will I be in five years
Not even a rhythm in her heart
Merely a dancer with the moon.

O my beautiful moon, it's been a week
since I saw you
Dance with me
To barbarian music
Forget the world
Feel the ecstasy
In the fog
Look at the horizon
Fall asleep.

Clowning
(To the everyday-boring ones)

Everyone drinks coffee
Everyone pops Viagra
Everyone masturbates
Everyone is polite
Everyone prays
Everyone donates to the poor
Everyone is on time
Everyone is in a relationship
Everyone lacks love
Everyone hugs teddy bears
Everyone has insomnia

Everyone dances in front of the mirror
Everyone is hurt
Everyone is funny
Everyone watches the 10 o'clock news
Everyone makes fun of Barack Obama
Everyone is vegetarian
Everyone is peaceful

Everyone is beautiful
Everyone is unique
Everyone is smart

Everyone is happy
Everyone is thankful
Everyone is positive
And I'm the clown.

TWO

American Haikus

(To Jack Kerouac, who made fun of poetry)

A regular day
some clothes and books
scattered on the floor.

Brown with a tall neck
kisses me with her sexy lips,
a bottle of beer.

Only rubbish in my room,
the yellow eye of the desk light
keeps staring at me.

A square mirror
a window
to the abyss.

No achievements today
just some scattered
Dreams.

A book of 200 pages
Empty words
Empty world.

It's not Christmas in New York
yet, the skyscrapers
are still awaiting Santa.

I don't know what the date is today
I still think
it's not my birthday.

When the night came
Her heavy eyes
sculpted lifelessness.

A solider stabs the sky with a knife
Eats his dirty socks
And doesn't thank God.

The sun has risen
We're high
on guns.

It's the last laugh
The sun is weird
And too bright.

Love
is an empty tobacco can
in the old lady's hand.

Other Haikus

Machine guns shooting
people dying viciously
Welcome to Baghdad.

Thoughts with guns and tanks
March, killing maliciously
Confiscate my heart.

Some peculiar walls
no color ... gazing, staring
Seeking nothingness.

Drips of agony
Draw the details of my face
They never noticed.

Night has come again
The typical hollowness
All gods went to bed.

Rainbows of colors
Wearing pitch black sunglasses
Blind angels with canes.

THREE

تحت الشمس

(إلى شمش)

أوشم أطراف أصابعك
برائحة الحرب
ولا تنتصر
أنت الذي سيموتون أولادك
بداء التنفس.

إحتج
لكي لا يتغير شيء
أنت الذي ستُسمع كل صلواتك
من قبل روتين المدينة.

أنظر إلى لافتات المحال
تذكر أن زاوية الشارع
كانت أمك الحنون
أنت الذي قلبك
أبرد من قصص الإنجيل.

أكتب رواياتك الحزينة
تكلم عن سخافة مستقبل المملكة
وعن ايديولوجية سياسة الثعالب
والتناغم البشري
أنت الذي ستكون فلسفتك
كشخير الله.

إقرأ الجرائد اليومية
إحرق غرائب الحياة
مع داء التبغ
أنت الذي ستنتهي مبتسماً
تحت الشمس.

Under the Sun

(From American soldiers to the God of Sun in
Ancient Babylon, Šamaš)

Tattoo your fingertips
with the smell of war.
Don't seek triumph.
You're the one whose children will die
with the disease of breathing.

Protest
so nothing will change.
You're the one whose prayers will be heard
by the routine of the city.

Gaze at the dark billboards
Remember your beloved mother,
the corner of the street.
You're the one whose heart is colder
than the stories of the Bible.

Write your melancholic novel.
Talk about the absurdity of the kingdom's future
about the political Ideology of foxes
and human harmony.
You're the one whose philosophy
is like the snore of God.

Read your daily newspapers.
Burn the oddity of life
with tobacco's maladies.
You're the one who will end
smiling under the sun.

انتظار

(إلى حروب الملائكة ... والأيام العادية)

حزن
وخرطوشة في رأس الهرم
إن الله تخلى عن الماء والوجود
تركنا لنلحق حقيقة الروايات الفارغة
ونتوه في السجل العام للأسماء.

حفرنا أدمغتنا بسيجارة
وضاجعنا زوجاتنا بصعوبة

ولم ينتهي الألم
ولا تجيب العراة

هدمنا أبراجنا العالية
وغسلنا أجسادنا بالقنابل النووية
حلقنا رؤوسنا
واستمرينا بالانتظار.

Waiting
(To angelic wars and regular days)

Sadness
A cartridge in the pyramid's brain

God has given up water and existence
He's left us to run away, chasing the reality of
stupid novels
He's left us lost in the public list of names.

We've drilled our brains with cigarettes
We've hardly penetrated our wives

The pain is endless
The wailing of the naked is endless.

We've demolished our high towers
We've washed our bodies with nuclear bombs
Shaved our heads
And kept waiting.

مملكة الله

(إلى فادي الصائغ، المجنون المختبئ)

كان صليبك عقياً
لا يكتب الشعر.
في مؤخرة جمجمتك
حروب كثيرة.
بارود.
قصيدة حب.
نهر ترابي.
أوشم جسدك حتى الموت
أكفر حتى تسكر القصيدة.
في كل عقب سيجارة إصلب فكرة جديدة
وتذكر أن الكثير من الكحول سوف ينهي آلام الملائكة.
قريباً ...
سنؤلف موسيقى الصراخ
وسوية سنقرأ قصص التائهين
ونحرق لوحاتنا السريالية
ونكتب لكل غيمة قصيدة سوداوية
وسنصلي ليذكرنا الله في ملكوته.

Kingdom of God
(To Fady Alsaegh, the hidden mad man)

Your cross was futile,
doesn't write poetry.
In your skull many wars were found.
Gun powder.
A love song.
A dusty river.
Beautify your body with tattoos 'til it dies.
Curse God and leave the poem intoxicated.
In every cigarette, crucify a new idea
and remember that alcohol will end the pain of angels.

Soon...
We will compose the music of screaming
Together we will read the stories of the lost
We will burn all of our surreal paintings
We will write for every cloud a dark poem
and will pray so God will remember us in his kingdom.

ادمغة مفتوحة

(إلى النهاية اللطيفة)

الدماغ مفتوح
لثقب الرصاصة المبتسم.

وفي الإشراقات
تسأم الشمس
والأطفال تُعجن
بدون محبة
والشباب يدخن الحشيش بكثرة.

الشريط الأسود
على صور القتلى
والكوابيس المستمرة عن الحرية،
كلها تصب في جوعٍ آخر
وليلة أخرى
وأغنية سريالية لشاعر فقير
تتكلم عن هلوساتٍ لاتنتهي.

وداعاً
ليوم آخر من السعادة المفرطة في حبوب الهلوسة
وحماسة أخرى في أقراص الفياغرا

Open Brains
(To the nice end)

The brain is open
for the smiling bullet hole.

In the luminosity,
the sun becomes monotonic.
The children are kneaded without love
The youth is on drugs.

The black ribbons
on the photos of the dead
and the continuous nightmares on freedom
are poured into another hunger,
another night
another surreal song by a poor poet
talking about endless hallucinations.

Farewell
to another day of drugged ecstasies
and the short excitements in Viagra pills.

Farewell
to the rising smoke
from the mouths of the continuous wars
and the evenings of huge cities.

وداعاً
لدخان السجائر
الصاعد من أفواه الحروب المستمرة
وأُمسيات المدن الضخمة

وداعاً
للشقق الضيقة
والسعرات الحرارية
والكتب السماوية

وداعاً
لثقب الرصاصة المبتسم
في دماغي الجائع.

Farewell
to tiny apartments
to fat calories
to holy books

Farewell
to the smiling bullet hole
in my hungry brain.

ملل
(إلى دُب سكران)

متأثراً بصباحات رامبو الهزلية
الملل يحرق أجواء بغداد ومونتانا.
ليحتضر العالم
برمادية السماء
بأعداد الحوامل المتزايدة.
ليتقن الله الضحك
على أحلام الأطفال.
انا الغير مكترث
بالسلام العالمي
وملكات الجمال.
انا الغير مكترث
بالمدارس المظلمة
والشعراء الشباب.
انا الغير مكترث
بالتكنلوجيا الحديثة
وجوائز نوبل.
الحكمة
في مشافي الجنون
النهاية
في الإبتسامات الشاحبة.

Boredom
(To a drunk bear)

Influenced by the comic mornings of Rimbaud
Boredom burns the sky of Baghdad and Montana.

Let the world die
With the grey sky
and the increasing numbers of pregnancies.

Let God master laughing
at children's dreams.

I'm not interested in
world peace, in
beauty queens.

I'm not interested in
the dark classrooms, in
young poets.

I'm not interested in
modern technology, in
Nobel Prizes.

Wisdom
is in the insane asylums
The end
is in the everyday-pale smiles.

ACKNOWLEDGMENTS

Tyson Habein
Sara Habein
Ziad Al-Shamsie

Special thanks to Fady Alsaegh,
who inspired me to write.

Originally from Iraq, Saif Alsaegh currently lives in The United States. After a youth spent in Baghdad listening to rock music and reading Arabic, French, and American writers, he continued his education in Damascus, New York, California, and Montana while writing and performing poetry in both Arabic and English. His work has appeared in *Witness*, *The Great Falls Tribune*, *The Legendary*, and other venues.

Iraqi Headaches is his first poetry collection.